Sojourner Truth

A Path to Freedom

Debra J. Housel

Consultant

Glenn Manns, M.A.
Teaching American History Coordinator
Ohio Valley Educational Cooperative

Publishing Credits

Dona Herweck Rice, *Editor-in-Chief*; Lee Aucoin, *Creative Director*; Conni Medina, M.A.Ed., *Editorial Director*; Jamey Acosta, *Associate Editor*; Neri Garcia, *Senior Designer*; Stephanie Reid, *Photo Researcher*; Rachelle Cracchiolo, M.A.Ed., *Publisher*

Image Credits

Teacher Created Materials

5301 Oceanus Drive
Huntington Beach, CA 92649-1030
http://www.tcmpub.com

ISBN 978-1-4333-1604-3
©2011 Teacher Created Materials, Inc.
Reprinted 2012

Table of Contents

A Young Slave Girl

Sojourner Truth was born in 1797 in New York. She was given the name Isabella Baumfree. She was born a **slave**. At age 9, she was sold to a slave **master**. She had to leave her parents.

Slave children were often sold away from their parents.

Slaves being sold

Isabella as a young girl

Isabella spoke Dutch. Her new master spoke English. She could not understand him. So she did not do what he told her to do. He beat her many times. Then he sold her to a new master.

A sick slave falls down

Slaves were treated badly. They had no way to defend themselves.

Isabella grew to be six feet tall. She was strong. She worked hard, too. At the age of 16, her master made her marry a man named Thomas. He wanted them to have big, strong children.

Isabella wanted to marry another man. But her master said no.

Isabella and Thomas on their wedding day

Isabella took care of many children.

Freedom!

In 1827, the state of New York ended slavery. Isabella's master promised to free her early. But he changed his mind. So Isabella left. She went to Isaac and Maria Van Wagener's home.

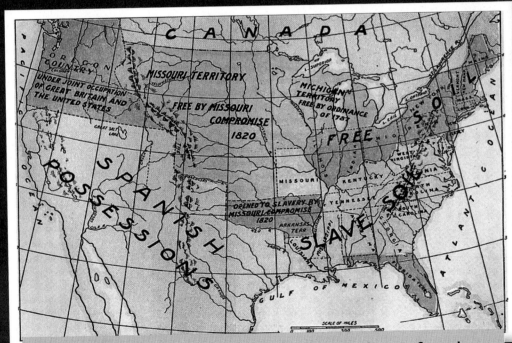

Many states ended slavery. This gave slaves freedom.

Some people who were slaves became free.

Isabella's master found her. Mr. Van Wagener gave him money to free her. Isabella worked for the Van Wageners. They treated her well. They paid her for her work.

Fun Fact

The Van Wageners read many books to Isabella.

Fun Fact

The Van Wageners were Quakers. They were against slavery.

A group of Quakers praying together

13

Going to Court

Isabella had five children. Three of them were still slaves for her old master. The master sold her son, Peter. He was sent to another state. That was against the law. So Isabella went to court.

Slave families were often separated.

15

Never before had an **African American** taken a white man to court. Isabella won! She got Peter back. She took him to New York City. He went to school there.

This school taught children and adults. Most slaves had never been able to go to school.

Fun Fact

Peter grew up to be a sailor aboard a whaling ship.

An old whaling ship

Isabella Changes Her Name

In 1843, Isabella had a dream. In her dream, God told her to tell the truth about slavery. She would become a traveling **preacher**. She called herself Sojourner Truth. Sojourner means "**wanderer**."

Isabella the wanderer

Sojourner Truth

Sojourner had very little money. She walked about 100 miles to Massachusetts (mas-uh-CHOO-sits). There, she joined a group of **abolitionists** (ab-uh-LISH-uh-nists). They were against slavery. Sojourner gave speeches for them.

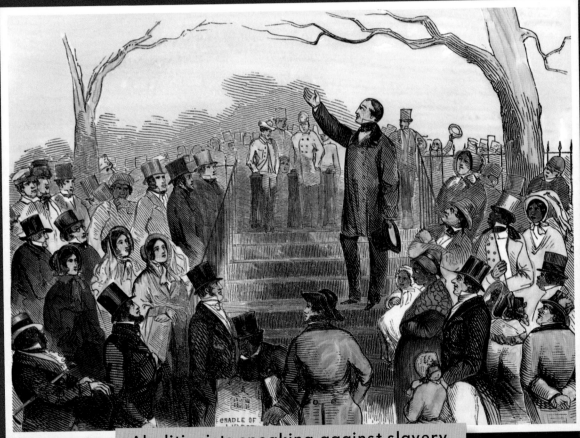
Abolitionists speaking against slavery

On May 28, 1851, Sojourner gave her most famous speech in Ohio.

Sojourner is ready to speak.

Crowds came to hear Sojourner speak. She gave her speeches in tents. Once, some men tried to burn down the tent. But she started singing. The men saw her courage. They dropped their torches.

Burning torches

Sojourner's bravery stopped the men.

Sojourner Changes America

In 1865, Sojourner got on a **streetcar**. African Americans were not allowed to ride. The streetcar **conductor** hit her. But she stayed on. She got the streetcar company to change its rules.

An old streetcar

Harriet Tubman

Like Sojourner, Harriet and Frederick fought against slavery and for equality.

Frederick Douglass

Sojourner often spoke about women's rights, too. She worked with famous **suffragists** (SUHF-ruh-jists). They were trying to win voting rights for women. Sojourner wanted all people to be treated the same. She worked hard to make this happen. Sojourner died in 1883.

Suffragists Susan B. Anthony, Elizabeth Cady Stanton, and Lucretia Mott

Sojourner visited President Lincoln in the White House.

Sojourner and President Lincoln

Time

1797
Isabella is born in New York.

1827
Quakers free Isabella from slavery by paying for her freedom.

1828
Isabella goes to court to get her son back.

Line

1843
Isabella begins calling herself Sojourner Truth.

1851
Sojourner gives her most famous speech.

1883
Sojourner dies at the age of 86.

Glossary

abolitionists—people who work to put an end to unfair laws, such as slavery

African American—Americans whose families first came from Africa

conductor—a person who operates a train or streetcar

master—a person who owns slaves

preacher—a person who talks about important things, such as religion and equality

slave—a person who belongs to another person and must work for no money

streetcar—a vehicle on rails that takes people through city streets

suffragists—people who work to win rights for women

wanderer—a person who travels around instead of living in one place

Index

Americans Today

Marian Wright Edelman is a lawyer. She was the first African American woman to join a group of lawyers in Mississippi. Marian works hard for equality for everyone. She believes that education is important. Marian's programs help children in America succeed. She once said, "You really can change the world if you care enough."